BREAKDOWN TO BREAKTHROUGH

Brenda J. Williams

BREAKDOWN TO BREAKTHROUGH

BREAKING THE CHAINS OF MENTAL BONDAGE

Brenda J. Williams

For the thing which I greatly feared is come upon me and that which I was afraid of is come upon me. [Job 3:25]

DEDICATION

This book is dedicated first to my Heavenly Dad, who healed and set me free. I also dedicate this book in honor of my Dad, The Late Pastor Milton K. Blackmon, and my Mom, Nadeen Blackmon, who made me who I am today. My parents are both my Heroes and True Pioneers of The Faith! They stood for God and fought the devil on every hand with the Word of God. My Mom taught me about Jesus; because of her, I received Jesus Christ as my Personal Savior. I invited Jesus Christ into my heart when I was about 6 years old. Through the Power of the Holy Spirit, I am alive today. I honor my daughter, Simone Williams-Young, who gave me a reason to live and was my daily inspiration! I am a living witness that the Word of God works! I also dedicate my book to my great-grandchildren and my awesome Son-In-Law, Reuben L. Young, who supports and encourages me in all my endeavors. May this book encourage you to walk by Faith and not by Sight! Just know that God will never leave you or forsake you. [Hebrew 13:5] Whatever you may face, you have the Victory over it! God is our Healer, Protector, and Deliverer!

ACKNOWLEDGMENTS

I am so thankful to those who helped me on my journey. You may have prophesied into my life, prayed for, or encouraged me during my trying time. Many of you did not know everything I was going through, but you were there for me, and I thank you.

Thank you, my daughter, Simone L. Williams-Young, for sticking by your Mom and loving me. You were just a precious and sweet little girl! You were so loving and dear to me. You would sit right next to me whenever you rode with me in the car. Sometimes you would kiss my hand. You gave me a reason to live!

Giving thanks In Honor of the Late Elder Bobby Smith, who received instructions from God to come and pray for me because the devil was trying to take my mind and send me to the Sanitarium. Thank you, Minister John Colbert, for praying with Elder Bobby Smith for me. Because of your prayer, God healed my mind.

Thank you, Treon Franklin, for the Prophetic Word that you gave me that the devil was going to try to take my mind, and it was going to be bad, but God really wanted me to stand! I thank God for your obedience! Every Prophetic Word prophesied to me, and my family came to pass! You are a true Woman of God!

Thank you, Carolyn Abrom, my dear neighbor, who listened to my dream and instructed me to see my Pastor immediately because the dream was very serious concerning my life.

Thanks, in Honor of the Late Pastor Floyd C. Miller for interpreting my dream and giving me the instructions to save my life. I also thank the Late Charles Maclain for immediately listening to my dream and contacting Dr. Miller. Dr. Floyd C. Miller taught about the Spirit World and how to deal with demons. Thank you, God, for them both.

Thank you, Kenneth, and Sherry Woods, for loving, protecting, and nurturing me. My Brother and Sister went through the storm with me all the way, even helping me clean my house free from demons. I could not have made it without you! I thank God for you both.

Thank you, Carolyn Lampkin, your son Desmond, and in honor of your husband, The Late Willie Lampkin, for taking care of my daughter, Simone. Monday through Friday, you picked up Simone from Elementary School, fed her dinner, and helped her with her homework for a while. You even fed me also! I could not have made it without you all. You were Angels sent from Heaven.

Thank you, Pastor Richard, and Pastor Shirley Adrian, for all the great things you did for me. You all provided God's best for me. Servants of the Most High God!

Thank you, my Dear Sister, Wendy McCuien, for all the delicious meals you prepared for me when I had surgery and for cleaning my home. We cried together from the pain I had after the surgery. You did not know everything was going on with me, but you were right by my side. You were an Angel from Heaven.

Thank you, my Dear Sister Dr. Geraldine Dotson, for opening your home when I did not feel good. You waited on me hand and foot. The awesome meals and care! You did not know everything that was happening to me, but you were right by my side. You were an Angel from Heaven.

Thank you, my Dear Sister, Carolyn Watson, for calling the County Pest Control and getting the rats out of my home. You handled everyone for me. I was under a lot of pressure! I cannot thank you enough! You were an Angel from Heaven.

Thank you, my Dear Friend, Mickey Thompson, for blessing my daughter and I while I was going through this. We were blessed with all of your hot meals and love from your beautiful daughter, Regina, and your husband. You all were Angels from Heaven.

In honor of The Late Dr. Helen Baxter, a true Prophet! I thank Dr. Helen for her prayers, encouragement, and prophetic words she gave me. Dr. Helen was always spot-on and very sensitive to the Holy Spirit. That one time when I thought I was not going to make it out of a dark hole, Dr. Helen called and encouraged me. I gained the strength to hold on! The enemy began to try to make me feel like my healing was not going to manifest because my healing process was very long. I rebuked those thoughts, and my healing did manifest not long after this. A lot of times, when you are tempted to give up, your blessing is right around the corner. You must continue to stand! I will never forget Dr. Helen! I believe Dr. Helen is among the great clouds of witnesses in heaven.

Thank you, Prophet Kendale Moore, for recognizing the book within me years ago and continually encouraging me to write my book. I can just hear you say, "Did you write the book yet?"

Thank you, Apostle Shana White-Smith of Diamond in the Rough Ministries, for also prophetically speaking into my life about my book from the Lord and your encouragement to get my book completed. You are an awesome Gift from God to me.

INTRODUCTION

Breakdown to Breakthrough (Breaking the Chains of Mental Bondage) is written to encourage those who may be experiencing any mental challenges. I went through a stressful divorce and found myself feeling devastated and betrayed. It felt like my heart had been broken into many pieces. I have heard people say divorce is like death because you become one with your spouse in spirit. I began to experience anxiety, nervousness, and depression. Fear had engulfed me! I was breaking down and on my way to the sanitarium, but God stepped in and healed my mind. The healing process was not overnight, but God brought me through.

Breakdowns come from different situations, and there are different stages! I am sharing my personal testimony of how God brought me through a dark time in my life, which strengthened my trust and faith in God. What the devil meant to destroy me with worked for my good

There is life after a Breakdown! You can be restored! The Lord is nigh unto them that are of a broken heart and saves such as be of a contrite spirit. [Psalms 34:18]

All things work together for the good to them that love God, to them who are the Called according to His Purpose. [Romans 8:28] Healing for some may be overnight. I stood on the Word of God, and God restored my mind. It was not easy! Allow God to take you through your healing process on your recovery journey.

When I held this Oracle in the palm of my hand, and as I began to read the pages that flowed from this book, "Breakdown to Breakthrough," I understood that this is a Manual and not just a book for those who may suffer oppression, fear, and anxiety which causes double-mindedness. Sometimes you may not understand how you ended up here and why God allowed this on your journey, but the one thing I did get out of this book is that even when the devil wants to make you feel like you are having a breakdown, God will give you a Breakthrough! We often do not understand "Spiritual Warfare," but Breakdown to Breakthrough will teach you spiritual tools and how to be the avenger still and fight by putting on the whole "Armor of God. You must believe and have faith in the Word of God! Read this book over and over! It will give you insight from God to break through your mental challenge through the Wisdom of the Holy Ghost. The Bible says in [Psalms 8:2]:

> Out of the mouth of Babes and sucklings has thou
> Ordained strength because of thine enemies that
> Thou mightest still the enemy and the avenger.

Jesus died to set the captives free! Get ready to receive your Breakthrough!

Apostle, Dr. Angela Roberson,
God's Handmaid

"Breakdown to Breakthrough" is an amazing testimony of God's faithfulness and His ability to break the Spirit of fear. The panic, anxiety, and confusion that often accompany fear can be paralyzing. This book will teach you how to overcome fear through faith in God and the power of His Word. So often, deliverance is not instantaneous. It has practical applications such as: confessing the word of God, praising God for the deliverance from fear, and confronting the fear - even when it means doing the very thing you fear. You will learn how to walk in your deliverance even when encountering resistance and spiritual warfare. Amazing testimony! Great book!

Apostle Joel Benjamin,
Author of Faith in the Blood

The Book "Breakdown to Breakthrough" by Brenda J. Williams is truly a weapon against the enemy. It is used as a tool to equip anyone seeking to obtain God's deliverance and healing from any type of mental health challenges. This powerfully anointed book shares how she became victorious from an abusive childhood and an unfaithful husband's lifestyle. It gives specific instructions and teachings on how to cope with fear, anxiety, and depression. Most importantly, it reveals how her Mom instilled the Word of God in her as a child, which gave birth to her breakthrough. Today, Author Brenda J. Williams is a strong, anointed Woman of God that has blessed the Body of Christ by being transparent in this book because it demonstrates how one can get a breakthrough using the spiritual tools in the Word of God. I encourage you to buy "Breakdown to Breakthrough" for yourself or as a gift to help someone get their breakthrough.

Dr. Betty Williams, D.D.

Breakdown to Breakthrough is a blessing to everyone facing mental challenges and should purchase this book. Breakdown to Breakthrough is a "gift-to-give" book, and is biblically based. "Breakdown to Breakthrough" is an inspirational tool for healing Mental Illness. It is an arsenal to halt the progress of depression, fear, anxiety, and Mental Illness. Brenda Williams is a powerful woman of God! With diligence, she crafted "Breakdown to Breakthrough" to infuse into many hearts of the mentally challenged to have faith in God and to trust in God and His Word. In sharing her life story, this godly woman underwent self-esteem-stripping experiences, but God carried her through. Through prayers, standing on God's Word, and Faith in God, God healed her from mental illness. God turned her trials into triumphs! Faith in God will heal many through this book. The source of this destructive mental illness by the devil is already defeated! Prisoners of Mental disorders are going to be healed and freed by God! "Breakdown to Breakthrough" is a book anointed by God! God will continue to bless the use of "Breakdown to Breakthrough" to dismantle the power of the devil to destroy the Mentally Ill. God will continue to use "Breakdown to Breakthrough" to ignite the hope for healing from Mental Illness! Breakdown to Breakthrough is for God's Glory! The "Power of God" rests upon it! "Breakdown to Breakthrough" will continue to herald that God heals Mental Illness!

Dr. NatiJesse H. Felipe-Guzman, Founder and President of Lord Jesus Christ *Int'l Outreach, Inc.*

This amazing book brought me joy! I recommend this book, Breakdown to Breakthrough, for anyone who needs encouragement! This book shows that God will never leave you, no matter what you might be going through. Breakdown to Breakthrough is a weapon for every believer who desires to be free from any type of Mental Health Challenge. Reading this book showed that Brenda Williams is an example of God being a Healer! This book shows the power of prayer and how God can give you joy during the storm! This book also shows that mental illness is not only real, but manifests through life experiences as an adult resulting from deep-seated roots stemming from childhood. Breakdown to Breakthrough plainly walks you through the Word of God and shows you how to receive authentic deliverance and healing if applied. This book also shows that there is nothing too hard for God, and all things are possible with God. This is an informative and life-changing book that will encourage, help, comfort, and support you during your storm. Breakdown to Breakthrough will not only show you how to deal with your fears or anxieties but will show that you can depend on God no matter what you may be facing at any given time. Breakdown to Breakthrough is simple, yet profound! It teaches you that you have the power and authority to take back your mind and peace and speak life through the Word of God. It also shows that through the Word of God, things must line up according to the will of God, and there is hope in God! I recommend this book to anyone who needs healing in their mind, body, and soul. You can use this book daily, weekly, monthly, and yearly basis and be encouraged and receive your healing.

Prophetess Temika McCann, AKA Coach T,
One Day at a Time Life Coaching

CONTENTS

CHAPTER 1

JOYFUL TIMES

I was born in Los Angeles, California, in 1952, during the time the Trolley Cars were running up and down Central Avenue in Los Angeles, California. Dad had prayed to God for a family and promised to take care of his family. Dad had been in World War II and the Korean War and had received an honorable discharge from the United States Navy.

Dad loved his family and worked two jobs to ensure we had everything we needed. Mom was a housewife, making our house a beautiful, warm, loving, and comfortable home. My Mom was born in Pigeon, Creek, Alabama, on a farm with 10 of her Siblings. Mom told me that they milked the cows and churned their own butter. They had many pigs on their farm and enjoyed plenty of fresh bacon and ham. Mom knew how to cook by helping her Mom cook for their large family. Mom cooked so good she reminded me of a Black Betty Crocker. Mom would make her Good Old Country Breakfast with Homemade Biscuits served with Peter Rabbit Syrup, or Homemade Canned Preserves. We also had Fried Chicken, Fried Rabbit, and Fried Green Tomatoes. Fried Rabbit is delicious! Dad's favorite breakfast was Filet Mignon Steak with Sunny Side Up Eggs. Mom also would cook Smothered Potatoes, Eggs, Pancakes, Grits or Hominy, and Homemade Alabama Sausage. Homemade Sausage made down in the South is the best!

Mom canned figs, pears, plums, and peaches during the summer months so we could enjoy them in the winter months. Mom also made plum and peach preserved jelly. Mom always had something good smelling up in the kitchen. When Mama made her Homemade Teacakes, Apple and BlackBerry Cobbler, and Sweet Potato Pies, the aroma filled up the whole house! Mom also made from scratch Fried Apple Turnovers, and Homemade Cakes. We had homemade goodies all the time.

We had a huge backyard where we created lots of great memories. We also had a huge Lavender Jupiter Tree in the middle of our backyard. I would often climb up in our tree and enjoy quiet time. The lavender blossoms from our tree would be all over the yard. It was a real task to keep the backyard tidy and clean. My Dad bought me soft sponge miniature furniture for me and my friends to sit under the tree. Mom often planned a Tea Party with little sandwiches and homemade tea cakes. Mom let me use my cute little Tea Set Dad bought me. Mom was the perfect Homemaker! Mom loved to make her children happy and enjoy being at home. Mom would wash dishes and watch us through the kitchen window, singing and smiling.

My Dad often brought home many pets for my brother and I to play with. We had chickens, hens, rabbits, and a dog. My brother had his own pigeon coop. I also had a pet pigeon named Polly. Occasionally, one of our chickens or hens would end up on the supper table. After we found out that one of our pets was for dinner, we would be sick for days. Our backyard was so huge that Dad installed my very own Tetherball Pole. My friends and I would run home and play Tetherball for hours after school. Years later, Dad built a new 3-bedroom home for our family in the backyard. It was beautiful.

I also remember going to the meat market on Hooper Avenue in Los Angeles, California, to get fresh meat. Live Chickens and Hens would be running around in the store in an enclosed glass display area. You would point out to the clerk which chicken or hen you wanted. The Clerk would clean and prepare your meat.

Mom was a beautiful homemaker and did crochets and beautiful embroidery on white dollies. Mom had her white dollies on the sofas, sofa chairs, and tables all around the house. Mom took time out to teach me how to embroider and crochet. My favorite was Mom's crochet house slippers. They were so cute, soft, and cozy! They hugged your feet and kept them warm! I remember my relatives coming over and getting slippers from my Mom, especially at Christmas.

Birthdays were special in our home. Mom cooked our favorite meal and baked us a Birthday Cake. Dad and Mom would always have a special gift for us. We all sang Happy Birthday, blew out all our candles, and made a special Birthday wish.

Christmas was also special, with lots of Christmas gifts under the Christmas Tree. On Christmas Eve, Mom baked all kinds of goodies for us and made her special Eggnog. This was the best time of the year! Dad worked two jobs to make sure we had everything we needed. We lived in South Central, Los Angeles, and every need was met. You could not tell us we were poor!

CHAPTER 2

DON'T ROCK THE BOAT!

On Saturday mornings, my brother and I did not go out and play early like other children. We had to strip all the beds and clean up the house. Dad was in the military, and our home was run like a ship. We had to keep our home immaculate! Captain Dad would inspect the house to determine if we would go out and play. My brother was two years younger than I.

We both had to polish the floors with old-fashioned wax that came in a tin can. We used cloth rags to apply the wax and then waxed the wooden floor in our living room down on our hands and knees. We also had to polish our beautiful French Provincial Wood Furniture. Dad had exceptionally good taste and took pride in our Living Room Furniture with a matching China Cabinet, Dining Room Table, Credenza Buffet, and two beautiful End Tables and Coffee Tables for the Living Room. Two beautiful Pearl Bottom Oval Glass Dome Lamps with Huge Round White Lamp Shades were on our End Tables. Our Sofas were covered in thick transparent plastic coverings to keep our sofas clean. This was the trend back in the day! Nobody was going to dirty the furniture! When I wore a dress, I remember how my legs stuck to the plastic when I tried to get up.

We had to clean out the window seals in the house except in our parents' bedroom. When Dad purchased carpet for the living room, my brother and I had to scrub the carpet with Dad's special cleaning solution on our hands and knees. We received orders from our Captain "Dad" to clean in a distinct way, and we dared not act like we did not want to do it! Dad could remove his belt faster than the Town Sheriff reaching for his gun.

Mom was a Housewife! Mom would make us do our homework daily, and we had playtime with our friends. Mom always read to us and encouraged us to read. Mom would make us write in cursive and check our homework daily.

My Mom, Brother, and I would be watching our Black and White TV when suddenly, Dad would walk by and change the TV Station quicker than you could flash your eyelid. Dad also did the same thing with the radio. My Brother and I loved listening to KGFJ, a popular black radio station with all the latest circular or "worldly music." Dad would not allow it! Dad would switch the channel to another radio station. We had to listen to Mexican Music. I love Mexican music to this day! My Mom would not dare ask him why he changed the radio station! Mom would just be quiet and sit there like a good little submitted wife. Dad loved us all very dearly but carried a big stick on his "Home Ship."

My Dad and Mom used to argue so loudly that you could hear them fussing outside when I went out to play. I would drop my head and be so sad just listening to them argue back and forth. This really hurt me! Mom was quiet in front of my brother and me, but she let him have it when my Mom and Dad were alone in their bedroom. It seems like they argued all the time.

We had a large garage. Dad's large brown liquor bottles lined up along the walls. Mom would send us out to play when we came home from school. I remember one day, a little girl came over to play with me. Before she came over, I took white cloth rags my Dad used to work on his car and covered up the liquor bottles. I did not want any of my friends to know that my Dad was drinking. When the little girl and I were playing, one of the cloths came tumbling down off the alcohol bottles, and I was so embarrassed! I could have just disappeared through the floor. Dad's drinking was taking a toll on me! I just kept covering up the liquor bottles.

CHAPTER 3

PANDORA'S BOX IS OPENED

I overheard Mom say he was not the same when my Dad returned from the navy. Dad was a little high-strung and nervous. The President sent out an edict that the navy had to serve an additional year even though their term had been fulfilled. My Dad was not a happy camper! There is no telling what my Dad had to go through in the two wars. This could have been why my Dad drank so much when returning from the service.

When I was about 6 years old, my Mom had been under so much pressure from my Dad that she had a Mental or Nervous breakdown and was admitted to a Mental Hospital. I remember Dad taking my brother and I to see my Mom on

Sundays. The hospital had a huge, tall chain-link fence that surrounded the hospital to keep the patients secure. Mom would sit outside with the other patients and walk outside in the hospital yard occasionally. My Dad would take me up to the chain link fence to see my Mom because children were not allowed to visit. My Mom would walk over to see my brother and me and visit with us. I knew she was not well from the way she looked, but I loved my Mom, and she would tell me and my brother that she loved us. I would be so sad when I left my Mom that I would always cry. I remember the big, beautiful Mumu Style Dresses my Mom would wear with beautiful Hawaiian Flowers. Mom also wore her beautiful Beige Patent Leather shiny shoes my Dad had bought for her. My Mom was a beautiful little woman! One wonderful thing my Dad did for my Mom was shop for her.

My Dad had to work while my Mom was in the hospital, and he would leave us with relatives. My brother, who is now deceased, and I were both violated when I was about 7 years old! My brother was 5 years old. We were around grandmothers, grandfathers, uncles, aunts, mothers, fathers, and cousins. My purpose was not to name the violator, but to pull the cover off the devil. A demonic spirit can work through anyone! The demonic spirit needs a body to work through, any-BODY! You think your children will be safe leaving them with your relatives, but that is not necessarily true! You need to pray and ask God if leaving your children with a family member is okay and pray about the babysitter. Lust Spirits, Unclean Spirits, Rape Spirits, Molesting Spirits, and Pedophile Demons are in your relatives also, Newsflash!!!! Your relatives will smile in your face and rape your children. This is why I would not let my daughter spend the night with classmates and other people. The devil also works through people inviting your children over to their houses for a sleepover. You must have discernment and ask God to show you people's intentions. Today you hear grandparents, mothers, and fathers raping their own children. We must be very careful, people! I cannot stress this enough!

The babysitter would take my brother and me into a room and do us all kinds of ungodly things. We were so little, but I never told my Dad or my Mom. I did not want my Dad or Mom to have a prison ministry. As I got older, I told my Mom something happened to me that was not very good, but I did not reveal what it was because it would kill her. My Mom never pressured me about it! This was an open door in Pandora's Box to other sexual behavior and desires in my life. People have major problems because of what happened to them in their childhood.

Mom got well and was able to come home from the hospital. It did not seem like Mom was gone for a prolonged period. I knew my aunt came over to help my Mom. Not long after, Mom began to take care of us by herself. We had our huge backyard, and my friends would come over to play with me and my brother. When I was a teenager, Mom told me that the little boys down the street used to come over to play with me when I was around 8 years old. One day, she went out to check on me, and I was butt naked. This was the first Episode after being violated. I do not know why my Mom did not talk to the boy's parents, that had come over to play with me. Mom just laughed it off! Little did she know that Pandora's Box had already been opened.

I remember we used to play hide and seek when we played house. Oh, there was a lot of sneaky stuff going on in our Playing House! We loved to play the role of Mommy and Daddy and, of course, sneak in a kiss or two!

I have other great childhood memories of playing kickball, tetherball, and handball with my friends in my backyard. I also loved to play football with the boys and hang out with my brother. I was a tomboy and loved to climb my tree in our backyard.

As I ventured into my teens, I was a very beautiful and slender young lady. When I would go over to a friend's house, there was lots of liquor and some men in the house visiting her Mom. The men would try to sweet-talk me. They would tell me how pretty I was and suggest they could buy me things. My

Mom taught me well, so I always managed to push them away and say no thank you. One of my other girlfriends that lived down the street would come over and smoke Marijuana in my friend's bedroom. She would ask me to smoke Marijuana with her, but I always said no. My little friend introduced me to lesbianism. Thank God I did not get deep-rooted in this activity! I was in love with the boys. Pandora's Box has opened again!

If my Mom knew I was being exposed to lesbianism, she would surely have had a prison ministry. Mom raised me in church and taught me good moral ethics, and the devil was busy undoing all my Mom was teaching me. This is why parents must watch and monitor what their children are doing. Things can happen right under your nose!

CHAPTER 4

WINDS OF FEAR PREVAILED

My Mom was a Godly Christian Woman who would always read her Bible, pray, and attend church. Mom would take my brother and I with her. When I was around 12 years old, the devil used to taunt me and say to me, "Remember, when your Mom went to the Sanitarium, you are going to end up crazy just like your Mom." This used to bother me so much! These thoughts would come and go. I would even end up sometimes imagining that I was going to die. The devil would show me my casket and funeral service; the next thing I knew, I would be crying. I went to church but did not know how to take authority over the devil and cast down these imaginations. The Church I attended never taught our authority over the devil. They never taught me that I could bind the devil.

> The Bible says in [Matthew 18:18]
> Verily I say unto you, whatsoever YOU shall bind on earth shall be bound in heaven: and whatsoever you shall loose on earth shall be loosed in Heaven.

Suddenly, by God's grace, I would snap out of the daze I would be in. I know this had to be God! The Spirit of Fear was torturing me in my mind. I realize now that this is where the Spirit of Fear entered my life. If you fear anything, the devil can develop a stronghold in your life, and you will be afraid of everything! When you get thoughts of fear, cast them down. You must get fear out of your life immediately! Do not meditate on evil thoughts, or they will go down into your spirit.

> The Bible says in [2 Corinthians 10:5]
> Casting down imaginations and every high thing that exalteth itself against the knowledge of God and bringing into captivity every thought to the obedience of Christ.

Speak to those thoughts and say, "I bind up all negative thoughts and cast you down in the Name of Jesus."

My Mom was a Virtuous Woman! Mom made our home such a beautiful and warm place to live. When Dad was in the Navy, Dad sent his money home to my Mom. Mom saved up all the money to purchase our first home. When Dad returned home from the Navy, Dad bought us a beautiful two-bedroom home.

Mom cooked everything from scratch and had me cooking and baking with her in the kitchen. I remember, as a little girl, I had a large notebook. I would write down all of Mom's recipes as we cooked. My Mom would say, "I am training you to be a wife one day." I loved my Mom very much and looked forward to our personal time together. My Mom had so much godly wisdom and loved the Lord with all her heart. Mom did not have many friends, so I was her best friend. We did everything together.

Dad loved us, but he was very strict! Our Mom would tell us she was going to tell our Dad when we got out of hand. We would beg Mom not to tell Dad. We would cry and almost get hysterical because we knew he would come home and whoop us in between Dad's two jobs. We would be so angry with our Mom for telling, but we did need to be disciplined.

When my Dad got upset with me, he would say, "you big old girl." He would also have a frown on his face! I was tall, and I would feel so crushed! I believe this is how the door of "Low

Self Esteem" opened in my life. Not only did I have to fight off feelings of depression, but I also had to fight off his ugly words. Parents must be careful how they speak to their children. Negative words create unhealthy images in their mind! Children never forget what you call them or how you talk to them. Words hurt deeply! Words can build you up or tear you down. We want our children to have a good and strong self-image. Be careful what you say when you are angry.

CHAPTER 5

TUG OF WAR

When I was around 15 years old, I had to sneak to have a boyfriend in Junior High School. Dad had been in the Military and did not want any boys in my life. I remember one day; I walked home with my boyfriend. The school was a mile away from where we lived. Walking to school was so much fun because this was the only time, I had to myself. I was raised with overprotective parents that would hardly let me do anything. I always had to take my little brother with me wherever I went. The other classmates could go to parties by themselves, but I could not. I had to take my little brother. My Mom would walk to the party and make us come home, and all the other kids would be dancing and having fun. The kids would laugh at me and my brother.

We walked with the same group of kids on our street back and forth to school.

One day when we got two blocks from my house, I saw my Dad's long navy blue and white Dodge Chrysler coming our way. It looked like a long Submarine Missile! I became frantic and said to my boyfriend, "I see my Dad coming this way." My boyfriend said, "Don't worry, I have this covered," he backed up into the crowd of kids walking with us and sat down outside a restaurant. My Dad saw me and him! He turned the corner and drove up! He beckoned me to get in the car, so I ran and jumped in the car. My Dad hauled me off, socked me in the face, and I saw stars! Dad said, "I saw you with that guy." He was so angry! Smoke was coming out of his ears! His temper could go from 1 to 100 in 2 seconds.

You would have thought I would have stopped seeing this guy, but I did not. My boyfriend really was not the kind of guy I should be around. This guy went to a Reform school for young men who had been in trouble. I was such a beautiful young lady, tall and slender. The boys always used to be after me, and I loved the attention! I became very angry because my Dad did not want me to have a boyfriend, and all the other girls at school had a boyfriend. I used to think about running away. It seemed like every time I would make plans, God would remove the thoughts from my mind. Thank God he did!

There is no telling what would have happened to me! My Dad would be mean to me, and I remember always rolling my eyes at him.

When I entered High School, I really wanted a boyfriend. I wanted to be like the other girls at school. I could not have a boyfriend until I was in the twelfth grade. It was Prom, and I wanted to go with my boyfriend. I told my Mom I had a boyfriend and wanted to go to the Prom. My Dad was so worried that I would get pregnant! Thank God the Doctor put me on birth control pills due to my horrible menstrual cramps every month. This was the only thing that relieved my Dad, and he let me go to the Prom. I went with another couple, and we had a great time. My girlfriend and I were very promiscuous with our boyfriends that night.

This was a night I thought I would never forget being intimate with my boyfriend; I really was let down because it was not what I thought it would be! I kept this a secret too! Dad had great intuition, though! I know he just wanted to protect me. I did take advantage of the situation! Pandora's Box has opened again.

After my High School Graduation, my Dad blessed me with a 1968 Orange and Black Striped Camaro Racing Car. I was shocked that Dad bought me this hot rod car to go to college. I thought I was a racecar driver, so this was not good! Working a part-time job during the day and going to college at night was great. I still had to go to church, of course. Dad still did not like me to wear makeup brought up in the church. Dad was so strict! I remember one day, I came to church with makeup on and dressed up in a cute dress I had worked for and purchased. Dad was the Pastor of the Church and sent me home. He told me to wash off all the makeup from my face, put on a longer dress, and return to church. I was furious and rebelled! On purpose, I put on the homeliest dress I could find. I pulled my hair way back in a ponytail and really made myself look very homely. Dad called me at home and told me I had better hurry up and get back to church, or I would get a whooping. I was 18 years old, working, and Dad still treated me like a baby. Even members of the church looked at me strangely when I walked back into the church. They looked like, oh my God! What happened to her? I rebelled!

I finally could have a boyfriend in the 12th Grade. I remember going on a double date. Dad told me I had better be home at 12:00 a.m. I went to the drive-in back then with another couple. We were 12 minutes late coming home. We were flying down the freeway in my boyfriend's lowrider car, bouncing up and down. The car had hydraulics on it. We were flying so fast, and I do not know how we did not get a ticket! When I arrived home, my boyfriend walked me up to the porch. He asked me to kiss him. I said, "No, the neighbors are watching." He replied, "Nobody is watching; give me a kiss." I said, "Okay, first let me turn off the porch light so no one will see us." I opened the door, reached in, turned off the porch light, and kissed him. I came into the house, and low and behold, my Dad was sitting in the living room reading his Bible in his blue smoking Jacket with his gold watch on top of his sleeve. I had turned the lights off on him!

My Dad jumped up and said, "Didn't I tell you not to come into this house this late? I had a dream that something bad had happened to you." Dad punched the daylight out of me again in my face. I had on a brown and beige bell-bottom checkered pantsuit. I wore brown platform shoes. The heel was at least three inches thick and three inches wide. I also had on my Mom's Family Birthstone Ring, which had four birthstones. Dad punched me so hard that I almost flew underneath the bed, buckled all up. When I stood up, my four birthstones had come out of my Mom's ring and were all over the floor, and the heel came off my shoe.

Dad was about 6'2. After he hit me, he left and went into his bedroom. The next morning, he came into my room and said, "I am sorry for how I treated you. I didn't mean to hurt you." He said, "I had a dream that a boy was trying to hurt you, but from now on, you do not have to be home at 12:00 a.m.

You can come home later." Boy, was I happy about this news! You know I took advantage of this!

Whenever Dad and I were driving around in his car, and we pulled up next to a car with a guy in it, he would say to me, "You had better keep your face straight ahead." I did not want Dad to punch me in the face again, so I looked straight ahead. I was not crazy!

CHAPTER 6

GOD ANSWERS PRAYER

After graduation, I was blessed to get a job at an Insurance Company that provided benefits to Teamster members. After two years, this company opened a position for a secretary to one of the Account Executives. This was a Management Position. I was 20 years old at the time. I wanted to be a Court Reporter, and this position was the last thing on my mind. One evening a little Black lady that worked for the company stayed after work to encourage me to take the Secretary position for about two hours. There were not many African Americans working at this company in management. The lady and I were outside the company chatting in front of the building. She said to me, "Young lady, you have all of the skills to fulfill the Secretary Position because you are completing your Major in Secretarial Science in College." I could type one hundred words per minute and had excellent shorthand skills. She said, "baby, this is a door set right before you, don't let it pass you by." I said to her, "I wanted to be a Court Reporter, and this is all I had dreamed of." She said, "baby, you will be the first Black Person to be a Secretary in Management; this is a great Achievement."

I thought about It and decided to compete for the position. God blessed me to win the Shorthand Competition! There were 10 Candidates Caucasian and Mexican candidates. The test was in the evening, and all the Black Business Agents of the Teamster Union Locals waited after work to see who got the position. It was like an election!

After the Shorthand Test, the results came in. I beat all the candidates! I was awarded the Secretary Management Position. The next day I received well wishes from so many people. Thanks to God, I made History by being the first Black Secretary at this company. Black Business Agents from the local unions came down from upstairs in the Teamster Building to congratulate me personally. My Caucasian boss even told me later that people were concerned about the outcome of the results for the Secretary Position because I was African American. He said it was a very delicate situation! My Mom and Dad had been praying for me and were so proud of me.

On Sunday, we spent the entire day at church. The morning started with Sunday School commencing at 9:00 a.m. Church Service started at 11:00 a.m. We stayed for dinner after church. Mom and several other ladies of the Church would prepare dinner then we would attend the 3:00 p.m. afternoon Service. BTU, Baptist Training Union Service was at 6:00 p.m. Afterwards; we attended Night Service at 7:00 p.m. We were at church all day!

Never give up on your loved ones! My Mom prayed, and Dad is proof that God answers prayer. Even though Dad was out in the world drinking and hanging out in the pool hall, God visited him one day. After the encounter with God, Dad never drank again. God's hands were upon him, and he later became the Church's Pastor. Dad's Church became a beacon light in the community!

Our relationship grew over the years! Dad became my biggest cheerleader. He always took time out to talk to me and encourage me. Later I got married! Dad was so proud of me and walked me down the aisle. God makes things beautiful in his time.

Dad and Mom were able to help families in the community. Mom and Dad reached out to the homeless and provided food for those in need. They sold barbecue every Saturday in the church parking lot and paid off the church. On Saturdays,

Dad started barbecuing at 6:00 a.m. The Police Department, Fire Department, and people from other surrounding cities came to purchase barbecue. Dad sold out by 11:00 a.m. Dad's barbecue was finger-licking good! Mom made her prize-winning potato salad, and my brother and I helped. Dad gave away free barbecue sandwiches to the homeless people on the street. Mom always cooked a hot meal, and Mom and Dad would deliver the food, pray for the sick, and shut in. They also went to pray for the sick in hospitals. Dad did many weddings and officiated many funerals. Dad and Mom served faithfully in their church for over 30 years. They were true servants of God!

CHAPTER 7

ONLY GOD KEPT ME

After I graduated from college, I met a young guy at my cousin's house party who was handsome, nice, and intelligent. We hit it off exceptionally well! We dated for a brief time. We were very much in love! My Fiancée asked me to marry him, and I said Yes! My Fiancée was so close to his grandmother and aunt that he could do no wrong in their eyes; he was so spoiled! They waited on him hand and foot! When we visited them for Sunday Dinner, nobody could sit in his seat, or they would get in hot water with his grandmother and aunt.

I saw red flags with my Fiancé, but I was in love and ignored the signs. I also wanted to hurry up and get out of the house! We were married shortly thereafter! We were married for 13 years. It just did not work out! I found out my husband was being unfaithful to me in the worst way, and things started going downhill from there. I tried to pretend to my husband that he was not hurting me, but it was. It almost crushed me when my husband told me he was leaving me. I hid this from my parents and everyone and acted like nothing was happening between us. This was not good! I was in denial, and later, this made me terribly ill.

The devil tried to take my mind when my brother was shot and killed. The Lord had given me a dream that someone in my immediate family was going to pass away. My cousin and I both worked for the same company at the time. One day my cousin came into my office very nervous, and her arms shook uncontrollably. Suddenly she turned around and ran out of my office. I knew immediately in my spirit that someone in my family had died. My cousin returned in 15 minutes. I tried to comfort her, so I said to her, "God already showed me that someone was going to die in my family." Finally, she blurted out that my brother and cousin were shot and killed together. I screamed uncontrollably! As I was screaming from hurt and sorrow, my mind felt like it was leaving me. Immediately, I felt a hand on top of my head. I knew it was God! When I came out of my office, some of the employees were in tears. Some of the employees had their heads down on their desks. I then proceeded to go to the end of the hallway, where a small restaurant existed. When I walked into the restaurant, there were several people looking incredibly sad. My voice resonated through the whole first floor, but God kept me from losing my mind.

I remember the day when my husband left! His best friend moved him out! I was so hurt! I entered our big backyard and sat on one of my daughter's swings. It all seemed like it was just a bad dream! I tried everything to save our marriage, and nothing worked! My daughter was 6 years old. Thank God she was not home on this day! I Thank God my Girlfriend dropped by to see me. My girlfriend said that God told her to come see me. This was truly God! I needed her support!

I went on with life, but many things began happening around the house. Things began to get on my nerves! The house began to seem like it was very dark! In my office, there was so much dark brown cork on the walls that I just wanted to rip the cork off. I was beginning to get sick.

Remember, the devil always told me I would go to the Mental Institution just like your Mom. The Bible says, *"For the thing which I greatly feared is come upon me and that which I was afraid of is come upon me* [Job 3:25]*."*

Our home sat up on a slight hill. Amazingly, we had a huge tree in the front yard right on the side of the driveway. The tree roots grew under the driveway, and the driveway began to crack and buckle. The tree roots also grew under our sidewalk leading from the driveway to the front porch. The sidewalk began to break and buckle. I also found out that the tree roots had also become entangled with the main plumbing line that led out to the street. This was the beginning of other sorrows for me! This was so costly to fix! My husband had just left me, and I did not really have any money for repairs. I was just trying to survive with my daughter. The utility bills at my home were astronomical also!

When I came home from work one evening, I entered the kitchen. There was an awful foul odor coming from around the Dishwasher. The floor was soft in front of the dishwasher. I called my Mother-In-Law to find out if she knew of a plumber, and she referred me to someone from her church. The Plumber came over and checked things out in the kitchen. He said he would come over the next day early before I went to work and go under the house to see if there were any leaks from under the dishwasher. I told him that I would come home during lunch.

The next day when I drove up to the house, the plumber asked me, who was in the house? I asked him, what was he talking about? There was no one in the house! I told him only my daughter and I live in my home. He said I am sorry Mam, but I beg to differ with you there are people in your house! I opened the door of my house and went into the house. There was no one there! In the back of my mind, I knew something weird was happening in my home because I heard popping noises throughout my house at night when I tried to sleep. Also, whenever I went to pray at night, I could hear people walking on my roof. I knew this was demonic! I was not going to let the devil stop me! I kept praying anyway! God gave me confirmation through the plumber that there were demons in my home. God will not let the devil come upon you unaware.

> The Bible says in Luke 12:2-3
> For there is nothing covered that shall not
> be revealed, neither hid that shall not be known,

The Plumber told me that the floor was rotted under the dishwasher. He said "termites" had eaten up all the wood under the floor in front of the sink and the dishwasher. He said, "I do not understand this; there is no floor underneath the linoleum where you stand to wash dishes." He said, "there was no kind of support under your feet whatsoever." He said, "I am baffled mam! I do not see why you did not fall under the house." I then said to myself it was only God that kept me! The Plumber replaced the floor. God had supernaturally held me up with the help of the Angels, so I would not fall under the house. If this had happened, it would have been over for me!!!! God knew it, and the devil knew it too.

The tree roots caused three significant issues. Firstly, the tree roots were breaking up the driveway, and secondly, the tree roots were breaking up the walkway to the front steps of the house; thirdly, the tree roots had clogged the drains to the mainline in the street. Also, remember the Plumber heard people in my home, and I could have fallen underneath the house because there was no floor for me to really stand on. This was scary! The devil was trying to push me over the edge with all that was happening in my home."

"After all these repairs, I called my husband and told him, "If he wanted the house, he could have it." I further went on to say, "I was sick and tired of all the things that were happening to the house, and I could not afford the upkeep." I told him that he could have the house if he wanted to buy it. Around five minutes later, I heard the Lord speak to me and say, "Don't do that, Brenda." I called my husband back and told him, "I did not mean what I said, and the house was not for sale." I was just stressing out." He said, "okay, no problem."

Now I began to have serious pelvic pain, and walking long distances was hard. Our Church was located on a corner at a traffic signal. When I went to church, I parked in our parking lot across and down the street from the church. I could hardly make It, but I prayed and walked by Faith. It was painful to even walk around the office at work. I was like, "God, you must carry me because it is just too much on top of everything else." My stomach also began to swell! I went to church one Sunday, and the Pastor said, "if we did not know Brenda's walk with the Lord, we would think she was three months pregnant." I informed the Pastor afterward that I had Fibroids and must have surgery to remove them.

I still had to press through until I had the surgery. One day I dropped my daughter off at school and met a lady living down the street from me. She said that her son and my daughter were good friends and played very well together at school. We chatted a little bit, and she said to me, "why don't you let me take your daughter home with us after school, we live right up the street from you, and we will see that your daughter does her homework daily and get her fed for you." We discussed that I was a single parent with a full-time job. I felt good about it after talking with her. She was a Court Reporter for the Superior Court and got off from work at 3 p.m. She was right downtown from the children's school. I had seen this lady and her husband dropping their son off and picking him up from school for a while. I paid her a visit, and we discussed it further, and I told her that would work out perfectly for me and this would be a blessing while I was going through my health challenge. In my spirit, they seemed like beautiful people.

> The Bible says in [1 Corinthians 10: 13]
> There hath no temptation taken you but such as is
> Common to man, but God is Faithful, who will not suffer
> you to be tempted above that you are able; but will
> with the temptation also make a way of escape, that you
> may be able to bear it.

God sent this couple to help me during my rough time. They fed my daughter, helped her with her homework, and when I came to pick her up, they made dinner for me, also. All I had to do was go home and go to bed. I needed to get off my feet with the pain from the uterine fibroids. God is so good! God will send you relief! God knows how much you can bear.

Several weeks went by, and I was scheduled for surgery. I had my daughter stay with her Dad. After I had my surgery, I was told by the doctor that he found a Fibroid as large as a grapefruit, and all the fibroids inside of me had burst. My God, if I had not been confessing my healing scriptures and standing on the Word of God, who knows what would have happened to me? God Kept Me!

I had returned home from surgery, and I still had to deal with all the problems that needed to be fixed at home. After a couple of weeks, I noticed I began to feel very nervous. My eyes began to twitch and would not stop.

I finally called a Word of Faith Church and asked for a referral from a Christian doctor who knew about Spiritual Warfare. The church gave me a referral of one of their doctors on staff to their Pastor. This was a huge Word of Faith Ministry. I made an appointment and asked the doctor if he was familiar with Spiritual Warfare. He said, "very much so." The Doctor did not like all the symptoms I was experiencing when he checked me out. He asked why you waited so long to come in and get checked out. I said I was just trying to deal with everything. I told the Doctor my husband had left me, and my house had so many problems that things were just getting to me. He prescribed valium and Librium for me and told me to return in two weeks. He said to make sure you come back so he could monitor me closely. He was overly concerned! I was still off from work, so I tried to rest, but I was becoming more nervous and anxious.

I received a phone call from an Elder at the church who said God showed him what I was going through. He wanted to come with another minister from the Church to pray for me. I told him they could come.

The Bible says in [James 5:14, 15]
Is there any sick among you? Let them call for the Elders of the Church; and let them pray over him anointing him with oil in the Name of the Lord. And the Prayer of **FAITH,** shall save the sick, And the Lord shall raise him up; and if he has committed sins, they shall be forgiven him.

The Elders came immediately! My Mom let the Elders in. One of the Elders told me about the Word from the Lord he received for me. He said, "God said the Devil was trying to give me a Mental Breakdown," but they are going to pray for me. He said God showed me you were headed for the Sanitarium, but God is going to heal you. The devil kept telling me I was going to the sanitarium like my Mom!

The Bible says in [Job 3:25]
For the thing which I greatly feared is come upon me, and that which I was afraid of is come upon me.

I had this worry and fear inside me from a young girl, and the devil was trying to make it come true. The Elders from the church prayed for me. He gave me some scriptures to speak against fear. He said he would give me more scriptures when I came to the Church.

After they prayed, it seemed like I got worse. I just wanted to lay in bed and not get up. I was depressed over everything going on with the house. The Holy Spirit spoke to me and said, "get up out of that bed." I felt oppressed and mentally heavy in my head. It felt like someone had stuck a sword in my head; I was nervous and fearful. My thoughts were confused! I got out of bed like God told me and started doing some work around the house. I was walking down the hall, and I stepped on a rat. The rat went one way, and I went the other! I was already dealing with the roots growing under the driveway and the walkway and roots going into the mainline all the way to the street, the floor rotting under where I stood to wash dishes every day, the popping noises that would go through my house at night; especially when I tried to pray, the nervousness and fear that was engulfing me and now dealing with my surgery for fibroids and now rats! I began to confess, 1 Timothy 1:7 - God has not given me a Spirit of Fear but of Power, Love, and a sound mind.

I called my Dad and brother to come over and put out traps for me. One night I was in bed and heard a rat trap go off. About 30 minutes later, I saw a mouse enter my room. I was holding onto my headboard! I was so frightened! I just happened to look on the left side of my bed, and the rat was sitting there looking at me. The rat did not move but just stared at me. I picked up my phone and called my husband, who had moved to Glendale, California, which was approximately 45 minutes away from Los Angeles, California. I told him to please hurry up and come because there was a mouse in my house. My husband knew how frightened I was of mice, so he felt sorry for me and came to help me. Let me tell you that the rat stayed in the same position and did not move!

The devil was really holding me in panic and fear! This devil was trying to push me over the edge! When my husband got there, he came in and hollered out to me, is the mouse still there? I said yes, this is crazy." He said hold on a minute, and I will be there! My husband came into the room with a trash can, scooped the mouse in the trash can, and took the mouse out. He said one of the mouse's eyes was bloody, probably from being braised by the rat trap. He said, the mouse probably was blind and did not even see me, that's why the rat stood in one place so long just staring at me. I was petrified! The devil was really running havoc in my home. My husband left, and I finally went to sleep after calming myself down. There was so much going on!

I went back to the Doctor, who told me he was sending me to the hospital to get a shot to help calm me down. The wrong kind of thought was flooding my mind. I was scared they were going to send me to the Psych Ward. I returned home after getting the shot. I tried to rest! I was lying in my bed, and I felt the movement of big trucks coming down the street on the ground, making me shake inside. I was so nervous and fearful! I just rested, took my medication, and tried to relax. It seemed like there was no solution! One thing just kept happening right after the other.

I was lying in bed, and God told me to get up out of bed and praise him. I began to praise him and give God Thanks. I was filled with the Holy Spirit with the evidence of speaking in other tongues. I would worship, and I would feel so much better. The oppression in my head would lift! I had to stay in worship to keep the pressure off my head. I had to cast down thoughts of fear and confess the Word of God out loud. Thank God for the Holy Spirit and my relationship with God that he would tell me what to do and remind me of what needed to be done because I would be extremely forgetful from the stress. I depended on God every day to help me do what needed to be done. God is real! This is why it is so important to be filled with the Holy Spirit with the evidence of speaking in other tongues. You can hear God in your spirit speaking from within. I cannot stress this enough!

My daughter stayed with her Dad while I had surgery and recovery time. My daughter had a very good Dad who always did over and above for her. He loved her very much. When my daughter returned home, I had to drive her to school. I had to drive to downtown Los Angeles for about 40 minutes. I would be so nervous that I developed a fear of driving on the freeway. The pressure was heavy in my head! It felt like somebody had stuck a sword in my head. When I walked around the house, I walked with my head leaned over because my head felt so heavy. When I drove by Faith on the freeway, I knew I should not have driven, but I drove anyway, shaking and trembling. The devil was not going to stop me from driving.

I just worshipped the Lord and prayed, and the pressure in my head would lift. I had to rebuke the spirit of fear, commanding fear to leave me while I was driving on the freeway. I would plead the Blood of Jesus over myself and against the fear. I had to get my daughter to school! I made it to her school every day, and I made it back home. My healing process was not fast, but I learned how to defeat oppression and depression by praising the Lord. I had to live for my daughter! I would look at her, and she would keep me wanting to fight and live. My daughter was such a precious and loving child. God knew to give me a little girl.

I had gone to see the Elder at church, and he gave me a list of scriptures on fear. He said to continue to confess the scriptures day and night until they get them in my Spirit. I also told him I began to feel so little when I would talk to some people. He said, "Through the Fear I was experiencing, I had opened the door to an Inferiority Complex Spirit." He said this spirit causes you to be afraid of people. There are many different types of fears. He said every time you fear a person, this engagement of nervousness is going to happen. The Elder said that I am going to have to learn who I am in Christ and build up my self-esteem. He said to confess scriptures on who you are in Christ.

I ordered a book we used in the Counseling Department at Church we gave to new members called "In Him" by Kenneth Hagin. In the book, he suggested that you go through the Epistles in the New Testament and everywhere you see scripture that referred to Jesus Christ in Him, In Whom, or Through Him, to write them down. These scriptures belong to the believer, and this is who you are in Christ Jesus. I confessed these scriptures out loud on who I was in Christ. I also meditated on healing scriptures as well as the scriptures on fear. I confessed all the scriptures out loud so they could get down in my spirit and build me up. I was buried in the Word of God.

> I would confess these scriptures:
> God has not given me spirit of fear but of power and of love and of a sound mind. [2 Timothy 1:7]

I can do all things **through Jesus Christ** who strengthens me.
[Philippians 4:13]

Be not afraid of their faces: for I am with thee to deliver thee Saith the Lord. [Jeremiah 1:8]

I was a total mess! I believed I was healed after the laying on of hands for my mind by the Elders of my Church.

The Word of God says in [James 5:14]
Is anyone sick among you? Let him call for the Elders of the Church, and let them pray over him, anointing him with oil in the name of the Lord and the prayer of Faith shall save the sick, and the Lord shall raise him up; and if he has committed sins, they shall be forgiven him.

I had received instructions after being prayed over, and I was going to be obedient and follow through with them. I had so much work to do, but I wanted my mind to clear up! I did not want to be locked up in a Sanitarium! Things were not going to change overnight, but I knew I had to keep confessing the Word of God, and the Word of God would destroy all that the enemy was trying to do to me.

.The Bible says in [Hebrews 4:12]

For the Word of God is quick and powerful, and sharper than any two-edged sword, piercing even to the dividing asunder of soul and spirit, and of the joints and marrow, and is a discerner of the thoughts and Intents of the heart.

One day I was at home taking my daily medicine. I opened the pill bottle for the valium and took it. When I opened the bottle of Librium, my hands began to shake uncontrollably. When this happened, it scared me! I said, "Oh no, devil, In the Name of Jesus, you are not going to get me hooked on this medicine." I got up and flushed the Librium down the toilet. I had no problems after this! My hands stopped shaking!

I was not a happy camper when my parents told me they were moving from Los Angeles to Rialto, California, sixty-three miles east of Los Angeles, California. The devil was still coming up against me with fear, so I really did not want to drive on the freeway. God knew I loved my parents, and nothing could stop me from going to see them, so I would drive out to see them having panic attacks and all. I would also have cold sweats! I would rebuke fear by speaking to it and commanding it to leave me in the Name of Jesus. I prayed in tongues and praised the Lord all the way down the freeway. The singing was calming to me, so I sang and made the drive. I confessed many of the scriptures on fear out loud and kept it moving. After a while, the fear finally broke, and I had no problems driving on the freeway.

The Bible says in [James 4:7]
Submit yourselves therefore unto God. **Resist the devil and he will flee from you**.

The devil will fight you with different attacks, but you have to fight him back with the Word of God and tell him it is written and speak the Word of God to the devil, and he has to flee from you in the Name of Jesus.

CHAPTER 8

KICK THE DEVIL OUT!

Get fear out of your life, or it will cripple you! One fear goes over into another fear. Some people are afraid to leave their houses and think something will happen to them. Some people cannot drive at night! Some people will not get on an elevator. Some people fear driving across a bridge; they have panic attacks and get off the freeway. Some people do not drive a car because they fear they will have a car accident. Some people are scared to get on an Airplane; this was another one of my fears! Some people have several drinks before they get on an airplane. Some people take sleeping pills. I would be afraid to fly on a plane and I would have anxiety attacks, but God broke that fear off me. I kept flying and speaking the Word of God to that fear. You must do what you fear! You must face it!

The Bible says in [Job 3:25]
For the thing which I greatly feared is come upon me,
and that which I was afraid of is come unto me.

I heard a well-renowned Word of Faith Preacher say, if you don't get rid of fear, it will go over into your life into other things. The Preacher said the way you come against fear is to do what you fear. There is no other way! What this Preacher said kept me going! I was not going to let the devil cripple me with fear of driving on the freeway or flying on an Airplane. Trust me; fear attacks everybody!

I would ensure I attended church because the Anointing of God was in the church. It is the Anointing of God that destroys the yoke of bondage on you!

The Bible says in [Isaiah 10:27]:
And it shall come to pass in that day, that his burden
shall be taken away from off the shoulder, and his yoke
from off thy neck, and the yoke shall be destroyed
because
of the anointing.

I Sang on the Praise Team and in the Choir. Some days I went to Choir Rehearsal, and I would be so bound up with knots in my back and in my shoulders. My head would be so heavy. I would sing, and the pressures would leave. The Holy

Spirit would lead me into praise and worship at home, and the symptoms would leave. After I kept praising and praising and praising over time, the devil had to flee. All that heaviness left me. I resisted the devil by doing what the Word of God said to put on the Garment of Praise for Heaviness.

> The Bible says in [Isaiah 61:3]
> To appoint unto them that mourn in Zion, to give
> unto them beauty for ashes, the oil of joy for mourning,
> the garment of ***Praise*** for **the Spirit of Heaviness.**

No one knew I was this sick except the Pastor, the two elders that prayed for me, another Elder, and my girlfriend and her husband. My girlfriend and her husband would come to get me and cook for me and wait on me hand and foot so I could rest. My girlfriend would not let anyone get close to me if she saw I could not handle them. She knew if I was getting distressed!

I used to sing the song, Humpty Dumpty Set on a Wall; Humpty Dumpty had a great fall. All the King's Horses and all the King's Men couldn't put Humpty Dumpty back together again. I thought I was so far gone that God could not put my mind back together again. I felt like I was lost beyond no return inside. I truly had to walk by Faith.

I woke up one morning from a dream. In the dream, it was like I was standing on the outside looking at what was happening to me in my own home. I saw a tall white man dressed all in black like a fireman. The man had a fire extinguisher in his hand. Standing in the house, I saw my daughter in her crib next to me. The fireman was spraying the whole room with the fire extinguisher and spraying the room from one side to the other, spraying my daughter and me. I knew that this meant the devil was firing all his arsenal against me and my daughter, trying to destroy us.

I then saw about 60 Cobra Snakes in a dark field with their heads lifted high above the ground with bright round green eyes and the rest of their bodies on the ground. I then saw myself walking on their heads. As I stepped on the snakes' heads, they disappeared. I saw this scripture in my dream magnified:

> The Bible says in [Luke 10:19]
> Behold, I give you power to tread on serpents and scorpions, and over all the power of the enemy and nothing shall by any means hurt me.

God showed me I had power over the enemy in the onslaught attack the devil was bringing against me. The devil was trying to take my mind! I told my neighbor that I had stepped on a rat and could not take it anymore living in my house. I also told her I did not know how the rats got into my house. This was the last straw!

I also shared with her the dream I had. She said Brenda, you have had a very serious dream, and I want you to call your Pastor right away. My neighbor was in ministry, so she knew about spiritual warfare and believed in demons. She said to make sure you call your Pastor in the morning. I told her I was not going home right now, so I went to my parents' home to sleep. I was just tired of the rats! I needed some peace and rest!

When I went over to my Mom and Dad's home, I went and laid down in my old bedroom to try and get some rest. For some reason, my Mom and Dad were arguing terribly. I tried to get some rest, but I could not. As I lay in bed, I could hear bumping from under the floor where I was sleeping. I went and told my parents about the noise. My Mom said, "it is just the dog under the house." I was like, oh my goodness, you mean to tell me now the devil has jumped into the dog, and the dog is making noises under my room in the house to buffet me. My Mom and Dad were arguing in their bedroom. I got up and told them that if they did not stop arguing, I was going to call the police. I did not like what I was hearing! Now you know it took all that was in me to approach them! When I spoke to them, they said you could just take yourself back home, so I went back to my house. At least it was quieter at my house. I had nowhere else to go! I had rats, but it was peaceful at my house.

The next day I called my Church and told the Assistant Pastor that I had a dream, and my neighbor told me to call and share the dream with him because it was very serious. He told me to come right in after sharing my dream. The Assistant Pastor said this was very serious; Brenda and I needed to call the Pastor to get advice on what to do. I was surprised but sat quietly while he tried to contact the Pastor. He said the Pastor went on a road trip, but he had his cell number. He contacted the Pastor and had me share my dream with him over the phone.

The Pastor said, "Who has a contract out on your life?" I said, "I do not know." He said, "You had better think because this dream is serious." He asked me how my husband and I were doing. I said, "We had separated." He asked me, "Would your husband put out a contract against your life." I told him, "No, he would not do that." The Pastor said, "There is something in your house that is giving the devil a legal right to come into your house and torment you." I told the Pastor that "Rats were entering my house, and there were popping noises at night in my house. I also shared with him that I heard people walking on top of the house when I prayed at night." He said, "The popping you are hearing in your house are demons." He said, "Are your husband's things out of the house?" I said, "No." He said, "Go through everything in your house and pack up all his things and have him come get them because there is something in your house he may have left behind that is giving the demons the right to attack you."

He said after your husband picks up his things, you are going to have to go in your house and get those demons out of your house. I was even more petrified!

I said, "Can't you have the elders and deacons come and get them out of the house." He said, "I could, but you should do it, Brenda."

> The Bible says in [Luke 10:19]
> Behold I give you power to tread on serpents and scorpions, and over all the power of the enemy and nothing shall by any means hurt you.

He said God gave you the authority to cast them out. This is the scripture God gave me when I had a dream. I saw the scripture like on a ticker tape! The Pastor said, "Take one of your friends with you and go into your house and anoint your house with blessed oil. Anoint the windows, the walls, the doors, the doorknobs, and the top of the doorways, and open all of your windows. Plead the Blood of Jesus in your house and command those demons to get out of your house." The Pastor said, "If you do not do it, Brenda, the demons can follow you wherever you go and always bully you around. Face them, use the Authority God gave you in the Name of Jesus, and command those demons to leave your house. They must leave in Jesus' Name."

> The Bible also says in [Philippians 2:10]
> That at the Name of Jesus every knee should bow of things in Heaven and things in earth and things under the earth.
> The Bible also says in [Matthew 18:18]
> Verily I say unto you, whatsoever you shall bind on earth shall be bound in Heaven; and whatsoever you loose on earth
> will be loosed in Heaven.

Demons are spirits and must bow to the Name of Jesus. They must obey the Believer that believes the Word of God. We have the authority to bind (apprehend, stop) their activity. We have the authority to cast them out and send them back to the pit of hell.

As I was going through the bookshelves on my Fireplace, I found a book I had purchased when I was in college that was pushed back behind several books covered up that said, "Mohammed is God." It was not anything my husband had left in the house, but what I had purchased myself gave the devil the legal right to cause demonic activity against me. I hurried and threw this book out because I am a Christian and know God's Word.

> The Bible says in [Deuteronomy 4:7]
> That you shall not have no other God before me.

I knew that Mohammed was not God, and I thought this must be the reason all this demonic activity had entered my home. I said out loud, "Mohammed is not God," "The God of Abraham, Isaac, and Jacob is my God, and he is the only true living God." I said, "I have received Jesus Christ of Nazareth as my Lord and Savior, the Son of the Living God born of the Virgin Mary who was crucified on the cross; was buried three days in the ground, and rose from the dead in the resurrection and is now seated at the right hand of God, I denounce this book, and I plead the Blood of Jesus over me." For this very reason, Christians must be careful what they bring into their house. You do not want to get under an attack from the devil, and you brought the attack upon yourself.

After my husband came and picked up his books on the weekend, my dear friends came over after Church on that

Sunday, and we followed the Pastor's instructions. We anointed the house, the doors, the windows, the walls, and the hallways with Blessed Oil and opened every window of the house. We commanded every demon in the house to get out. We said, "We plead the Blood of Jesus in this house, we plead the Blood of Jesus over this house, we plead the Blood of Jesus against every demon in this house." We opened the doors and commanded every demonic spirit to get out. My girlfriend said, "You can feel the house is getting lighter as we Plead the Blood of Jesus." There was a heaviness in the room. We kept Pleading the Blood of Jesus until we felt the Demons were gone and the heaviness lifted. That night I slept like a baby, and all the popping noises in the house stopped. No one was up walking on the roof when I prayed that night. It was total peace in the house. Thank God we got the demons out of the house, but we had not gotten rid of the rats in the house!

I felt impressed by God to reach out to a cousin that worked for the L. A. County Health Department. I shared with her that rats were coming into my house. She said not to worry; she would contact the LA County Pest Control to come out and check my property. Thank God the L.A. County Pest Control Department came out and checked the property completely. They went on top of the roof and found out that the covering to the Chimney was off and the Chimney was wide open! The rats were coming down through the Chimney into the house. There were many fruit trees where I lived, and the rats were eating pretty well! I also lived down from a huge open field which drew a lot of rodents into the neighborhood. I was informed to ensure everything was kept high off the garage floor. They put poison everywhere. Thank God we got rid of the rats, and I no longer have to walk on pins and needles in the house. You know I had them put a good screen on the top of the Chimney. Goodbye, rats!

I returned to work, still walking by Faith. I was able to do my work! I had a pleasant job and enjoyed my work. The place where I worked made dolls, so it was a very happy place. I enjoyed going to work! I worked in a small, enclosed cubicle, so I had peace. I still had to deal with thoughts of fear and anxiety. The devil was still attacking my self-image even though a lot of things had fallen off me. I kept confessing scriptures on who I was in Christ to build up my self-esteem. On my lunch, I read my Bible and reviewed all my scriptures on healing and fear. I had typed them up and kept them in my Bible. The scriptures were quite easy to access and review.

I was President of the Women's Fellowship at my Church. I did not stop planning monthly Fellowships. God continued to pour into me creative ideas for our fellowships. I knew I was under attack, but I believed God and continued to do everything I was called to do in the ministry. I walked by Faith and not by sight! I did not let the devil stop me. Remember, only a few people knew what I was going through. When some people came to my home, I did not let them in on anything. At one of the Women's Fellowship Meetings, the Pastor pulled up a seat behind me while I was sitting at the Head Table. He said he just wanted to share what God had shown him briefly. He said Brenda, God said that you had gotten rid of about 85% of the fear. He said Brenda, other people would have died from what you went through, but God brought you through. I knew that devil wanted me to commit suicide from the pressure, but I stood. The Pastor was just giving me encouraging words. I thanked him for sharing it with me.

I continued with my life raising my daughter and doing the work of the Lord by Faith. I got stronger and stronger, and my mind cleared up over several years. It took 15 or more years for my mind to completely get back to where it was before I got sick. I literally learned through all this that I had more power than the devil, and there is nothing that he can throw at me that God's Word cannot defeat. I also learned that the Power of Praise is a Weapon and will defeat and destroy depression and oppression.

During your healing process, Keep your mind on the Word of God. Talk to God about what you are facing and feeling. Forgive anyone that has hurt you. If you have unforgiveness in your heart, get rid of it so you can be healed. Let God deal with those who hurt you, but you release them. Forgive yourself also! We can sometimes blame, condemn, and beat ourselves down, which is not good! You need to forgive yourself! We are going to make mistakes in life! Some people may feel that God is punishing them for something they did! Whatever the situation, there is forgiveness! Ask God to forgive you and keep moving forward!

The Bible says in [Romans 12:19]
Dearly beloved, avenge not yourselves, but rather give place unto wrath; for it is written, vengeance is mine I will repay.

The Bible says in [1 John 1:9]
If you confess your sins, God is faithful and just to forgive us our sins and to cleanse us from all unrighteousness.

The Bible says in [Romans 8:1]
There is therefore no condemnation to those who are in Christ Jesus who do not walk according to the flesh, but according to the Spirit.

God will comfort you! God will also send people in your life to help you during your healing process. A dear friend, Dr. Apostle Helen Baxter, called me whenever I felt very low. Helen always knew when to call me! She would say things that would pull me out of some of the darkest times I went through. I thank God for Dr. Helen for crossing my path. I salute this mighty Woman of God that has gone on to Glory. Ask God to send you people to pray with you, love and encourage you. God knows what you are going through.

Stay in Worship and Praise. Keep Praise and Worship music continually in your home and car to keep your spirit uplifted. Get prayer for Healing! There are many churches that are Spirit-Filled, Anointed, and operate in Healing and Deliverance. Once you have been prayed for, Thank God for your Healing. Develop a personal relationship with the Lord. Be careful who you share your medical challenge with besides your Pastor. Some people will discuss your personal business with others! It is crucial that you pray and ask God who to open up with. Everyone is not confidential! Ask God to strengthen you to stand, and He will. If you need professional medical help, get it! God works through the doctors. Take your medication, eat healthy, and exercise. Stay around positive people that will uplift you.

A positive environment is very important! Keep your living space nice and tidy. You will feel better! A dirty home will bring you down and can be depressing. Keep things neat as much as you can. Often you may not feel good! The less frustrated you are, the better! You must do things to help yourself! Put up positive, uplifting quotes and scriptural plaques on the walls of your home to encourage yourself. Scriptural Plaques are a great way to keep the Word of God in your spirit. Just a few here and there. Keep fresh flowers and plants around you if you like them. Even flowers from the 99-cent store will cheer you up. Beautiful scenery pictures will also cheer you up. Put things in your home that will make you happy and put a smile on your face.

If you had a good childhood, put up memorable family pictures around the house that will bring you joy. Even a portable waterfall brings peace into your home. Scented candles are also good. You want your home to smell good. For some people, pets can bring you healing because they love unconditionally. It is good if you desire to get something small that will not be too overwhelming to clean up behind. We mentioned earlier that it is important to keep soft praise and worship music playing in your home. A Clean, beautiful home will help you stay relaxed. This is your "happy place." Keep people out of your home that are confrontational and negative. You want to relax in a peaceful environment during your time of healing. Surround yourself with prayerful and supportive people!

Know that God loves you! God is waiting to heal you no matter what caused the challenge you are facing.

> The Bible says in [Hebrews 13:5]
> Let your conversation be without covetousness,
> and be content with such things as you have: for He
> hath said, **I will never leave you or forsake you.**

God is here for you! God will never throw you away! Keep your mind on the Word of God! When my mind was confused, I kept myself in the Word of God. When I would read the Word of God, I could literally feel pressures leaving my mind. Your healing may not happen overnight! It took me over 15 years for my mind to clear up. I had to follow the instructions that came with the Prophetic Word that was prophesied to me. You must follow the instructions God gave you and do not deviate. I had to work on confessing healing scriptures, keeping my mind in the Word of God, casting down all imaginations, and walking by Faith. Once you are prayed for and have received your healing by Faith, you thank God you are healed. I kept confessing, "God, I believe I received my healing, and I thank you that my **mind is healed.**"

The Bible says in [Mark 11:23]

For verily I say unto you, that whosoever shall "**<u>say</u>**" unto this mountain be thou removed and be thou cast into the sea, and shall not doubt in his heart, but shall believe that those things which he saith shall come to pass; he shall have whatsoever he saith.

In my case, my mountain was my mind; your situation and mountain may be different. I had to say, mind; you are healed! Mind, you must get in line with the Word of God. I rebuke fear from me today. I command peace over my mind. I would say my favorite healing scripture throughout the day.

The Bible says in [Isaiah 53: 4,5]
Surely He hath borne our griefs and carried our sorrows;
yet, we did esteem him stricken smitten of God and afflicted.
But He was wounded for our transgressions, He was bruised
for our iniquities: the chastisement of our peace was upon Him, and with His stripes we are healed.

Stress kept falling off me as I spoke to it. Now, I am completely free, healed, and on fire for God. God did it for me, and he can do it for you.

The devil thought he could cause me to have a full Mental Breakdown, but God did not allow it! God stepped in and healed my mind! God gave me a Breakthrough! That's why my Book is called **"Breakdown to Breakthrough"**. God turned what the devil meant for bad in my life into my good. The devil tried to take my mind, so I could not preach the Gospel. After God healed my mind, God blessed me to become a Licensed Minister, and now, I am an Ordained Pastor Preaching the Good News of Jesus Christ that God Heals. I am a Living Testimony!

I am now a Playwright! God gave me a Stage Play to preach the Gospel to the lost and to win souls to Christ. The name of my Stage Play is "The Five Foolish Virgins." You can find it on Facebook. I am also a Producer and Director of my own Stage Play. I could not write for the Kingdom of God if I did not have my mind. God has much work for me to do. I am presently working on other projects. I also became a Caregiver for others and a Pastoral Care Chaplain for Loma Linda Hospitals. I returned to school and received my Bachelor of Arts Degree and Master's Degree in Theology. I was blessed to be a Co-Host on a TV Show for OCN Television Network. I am also a Singer, Songwriter, Actor, and now the Author of Breakdown to Breakthrough and more books to come. I shared this with you to see what God has done for me so you can be encouraged. It is not over! God is still in the miracle-working business! God has plans for your life, and none of God's plans include defeat.

> The Bible says in [Jeremiah 29:11]
> For I know the thoughts that I think towards you,
> Saith the Lord, thoughts of peace, and **not of evil,**
> to give you an expected end.
> The Bible says in [John 10:10]
> The thief cometh not, but for to steal, and to kill, and to destroy: I am come that they might have life, and that they might have it more abundantly.

God has great plans for you! God wants you whole! God wants you Healed!

God truly caused me to **Breakthrough** Mental Depression, Oppression, Fear, Anxiety, and Nervousness. Now I can help others get free through my personal Testimony. God is a Healer! Some people are healed right away! God did not heal me right away! God allowed me to use my Faith and trust him through my healing process. After you go through your healing process, you can help others! In your healing process, you learn that the Word of God works for you! You learn that God is with you! You learn that The Power of The Holy Spirit is in you. You learn to Trust God, and most of all, you learn that

God is with you every step of the way. **"*You Are More Than a Conqueror.*"**

There are scriptures on fear at the back of the book. Read, confess, memorize, and meditate until they get down in your heart.

Healing belongs to the Believer! Jesus is the only one that can bring you through Life's Challenges. You need God's Power! You need to get filled with the Holy Spirit with the evidence of speaking in tongues.

> The Bible says in [Acts 2:38]
> And these **signs** shall follow them that believe. In **MY NAME** shall they cast out "devils." They shall **speak** with **new tongues**; they shall **lay hands** on the sick and they **shall recover.** They shall take up serpents; and if they drink any deadly thing, it shall not hurt them; they shall **lay hands on the sick and they shall recover.**

You want to be in a Spirit-Filled Deliverance Church that believes in the Gifts of the Holy Spirit and operates in Healing and Deliverance. The Bible says ***you shall recover***! I used my Faith and believed God's Word, and I recovered. You can be healed from any mental challenges, sickness, or disease that tries to destroy you. God wants you whole! God wants you to live! Jesus has paid the price on the cross at Calvary!

The Bible says in [Hebrews 10:25]

Not forsaking the assembling of ourselves together, as the manner of some is: but exhorting one another: and so much the more as you see the day approaching.

Pray and ask God to lead you to the right church, and he will. Going to Bible Study will help build your Faith and Trust in God. It is the Anointing that destroys the bondages and yokes in our life. The Word of God heals and builds you up! Also, pick up books on Healing in your local Christian Bookstore, or you may order books on healing through Amazon.com. Allow books on healing to feed your spirit while you are going through your healing process.

The Bible says in [Romans 10: 9, 10]

If you confess with your mouth, and believe in your Heart that God has raised Jesus Christ from the Dead you shall be saved for with the heart confession is made unto salvation.

If you want to receive Jesus Christ as your personal **Lord** and **Savior** please say the prayer below out loud wherever you are:

Salvation Prayer

Dear God, I receive your Son Jesus Christ into my life right now as my Lord and my Savior. I confess that Jesus Christ was born of the Virgin Mary, He was buried in the ground for 3 days, and he was raised from the dead. Jesus is now seated at the right hand of God. I ask you to forgive me of of all my sins. I give you my life, my soul, and my body. I denounce the devil and all other Gods I may have worshipped. I thank you, God I am now saved in Jesus' Name.

If this book blessed you, I would like to hear from you:
Email Address: Authorbrendajwilliams@gmail.com

(Available for Speaking Engagements, Book Readings, Women's Conferences and Retreats.)

Home Church:
Chief Apostle Michael L. Rowles, Senior Pastor
The Wrecking Crew for Christ Holiness Church
11250 Avalon Boulevard
Los Angeles, CA 90061
Sunday Worship Service 11:30 a.m.
Sunday Night Service 7:00 p.m.
Thursday Night Service 7:00 p.m.

SCRIPTURES ON FEAR

Isaiah 41:10 Fear not, for I am with you; be not dismayed, for I am your God; I will strengthen you, I will help you, I will uphold you with my righteous right hand.

2 Timothy 1:7 For God gave us a spirit not of fear but of power and love and A SOUND MIND.

1 John 4:18 There is no fear in love, but perfect love casts out fear. For fear has to do with punishment, and whoever fears has not been perfected in love.

Psalm 34:4 I sought the LORD, and he answered me and delivered me from all my fears.

Proverbs 29:25 The fear of man lays a snare, but whoever trusts in the LORD is safe.

Joshua 1:9 Have I not commanded you? Be strong and courageous. Do not be frightened, and do not be dismayed, for the LORD your God is with you wherever you go.

Psalm 23:1-6 A Psalm of David. The LORD is my shepherd; I shall not want. He makes me lie down in green pastures. He leads me beside still waters. He restores my soul. He leads me in paths of righteousness for his name's sake. Even though I walk through the valley of the shadow of death, I will fear no evil, for you are with me; your rod and your staff, they comfort me. You prepare a table before me in the presence of my enemies; you anoint my head with oil; my cup overflows.

Psalm 56:3-4 When I am afraid, I put my trust in you. In God, whose word I praise, in God I trust; I shall not be afraid. What can flesh do to me?

Philippians 4:6 Do not be anxious about anything, but in everything by prayer and supplication with thanksgiving let your requests be made known to God.

Deuteronomy 31:6 Be strong and courageous. Do not fear or be in dread of them, for it is the LORD your God who goes with you. He will not leave you or forsake you.

Psalm 27:1 The LORD is my light and my salvation; whom shall I fear? The LORD is the stronghold of my life; of whom shall I be afraid?

Romans 8:15 For you did not receive the spirit of slavery to fall back into fear, but you have received the Spirit of adoption as sons, by whom we cry, "Abba! Father!

John 14:27 Peace I leave with you; my peace I give to you. Not as the world gives do I give to you. Let not your hearts be troubled, neither let them be afraid.

Psalm 23:4 Even though I walk through the valley of the shadow of death, I will fear no evil, for you are with me; your rod and your staff, they comfort me.

Romans 8:38-39 For I am sure that neither death nor life, nor angels nor rulers, nor things present nor things to come, nor powers, nor height nor depth, nor anything else in all creation, will be able to separate us from the love of God in Christ Jesus our Lord.

1 Peter 5:6-7 Humble yourselves, therefore, under the mighty hand of God so that at the proper time he may exalt you, casting all your anxieties on him, because he cares for you.

Philippians 4:6-7 Do not be anxious about anything, but in everything by prayer and supplication with thanksgiving let your requests be made known to God. And the peace of God, which surpasses all understanding, will guard your hearts and your minds in Christ Jesus.

Psalm 118:6 The LORD is on my side; I will not fear. What can man do to me?

Psalm 111:10 The fear of the LORD is the beginning of wisdom; all those who practice it have a good understanding. His praise endures forever!

Matthew 10:28 And do not fear those who kill the body but cannot kill the soul. Rather fear him who can destroy both soul and body in hell.

Isaiah 41:13 For I, the LORD your God, hold your right hand; it is I who say to you, "Fear not, I am the one who helps you."

Matthew 6:34 "Therefore do not be anxious about tomorrow, for tomorrow will be anxious for itself. Sufficient for the day is its own trouble.

Isaiah 43:1-3 But now thus says the LORD, he who created you, O Jacob, he who formed you, O Israel: "Fear not, for I have redeemed you; I have called you by name, you are mine. When you pass through the waters, I will be with you; and through the rivers, they shall not overwhelm you; when you walk through fire you shall not be burned, and the flame shall not consume you. For I am the LORD your God, the Holy One of Israel, your Savior. I give Egypt as your ransom, Cush and Seba in exchange for you.

Isaiah 35:4 Say to those who have an anxious heart, "Be strong; fear not! Behold, your God will come with vengeance, with the recompense of God. He will come and save you."

1 Peter 3:14 But even if you should suffer for righteousness' sake, you will be blessed. Have no fear of them, nor be troubled,

Hebrews 13:6 So we can confidently say, "The Lord is my helper; I will not fear; what can man do to me?"

Deuteronomy 3:22 You shall not fear them, for it is the LORD your God who fights for you.

Psalm 27:1-14 The LORD is my light and my salvation; whom shall I fear? The LORD is the stronghold of my life; of whom shall I be afraid? When evildoers assault me to eat up my flesh, my adversaries, and foes, it is they who stumble and fall. Though an army encamp against me, my heart shall not fear; though war arise against me, yet I will be confident. One thing have I asked of the LORD, that will I seek after: that I may dwell in the house of the LORD all the days of my life, to gaze upon the beauty of the LORD and to inquire in his temple. For he will hide me in his shelter in the day of trouble; he will conceal me under the cover of his tent; he will lift me high upon a rock.

Psalm 91:1-16 He who dwells in the shelter of the Most High will abide in the shadow of the Almighty. I will say to the LORD,

"My refuge and my fortress, my God, in whom I trust." For he will deliver you from the snare of the fowler and from the deadly pestilence. He will cover you with his pinions, and under his wings, you will find refuge; his faithfulness is a shield and buckler. You will not fear the terror of the night, nor the arrow that flies by day.

Mark 5:36 But overhearing what they said, Jesus said to the ruler of the synagogue, "Do not fear, only believe."

Psalm 56:3 When I am afraid, I put my trust in you.

Printed in the USA
CPSIA information can be obtained
at www.ICGtesting.com
LVHW010449060424
776629LV00047B/412